CHIMPS

by Jane Goodall

A Byron Preiss Book
iBooks for Young Readers
Habent Sua Fata Libelli

◇ Introduction: The Chimpanzees by Jane Goodall

I have spent most of my life studying chimpanzees. I began in 1960 when people knew almost nothing about how they live in the wild. I shall always remember arriving at the Gombe National Park to begin my chimpanzee research. I was twenty-three years old and the authorities refused to allow a young English girl to go into the bush by herself. I had to chose a companion—so my mother came. After three months I was beginning to feel at home in the mountains and forests of the chimpanzee's home. My mother had to return to England, but by then everyone realized that I could look after myself.

Every morning I got up at five-thirty and set off to search for chimps. But even when I found some they were so shy that they moved off when they saw me. There were times when I thought I would never be accepted by them. However, I found a wonderful hilltop overlooking two valleys and watched the chimps from there, through binoculars. Gradually I learned more and more about the way they lived—and they got used to me and realized I was not so frightening after all.

The first chimpanzee who learned to trust me was one I called David Greybeard. He came to my camp for the ripe palm nuts growing there and found some bananas. He came again, and he brought others with him—his friends Goliath and William, and then old Flo and her family and many others. And so, after a year, I was able to get quite close to the chimps when I found them in the forest. I watched what they did and wrote down my observations in my little notebooks.

I started the study on my own, but soon I needed people to help. Today a team of Tanzanian field assistants keep up the daily records. They follow a different chimpanzee each day. Every chimpanzee has his or her own personality, just as we do. They look different from each other, and they behave differently too. We write down information about each one so that eventually we shall have a collection of life histories.

As you read this book you will see that chimpanzees are like us in many ways, and this makes them particularly fascinating to study. I expect to continue observing the Gombe chimpanzees for the rest of my life and hope that the study will continue after I have gone.

◇ Contents

◇ Where Do Chimpanzees Live?

Chimpanzees live in forests that stretch across western and central Africa. In some places, where it is very wet, these are thick, tropical rain forests, almost jungles. In other places there are strips of dense forest along the rivers, with woodland and even open grassland in between. The chimpanzees do not feel safe when they move away from trees, and usually cross open ground in groups, travelling without stopping until they reach the trees again.

In most places where chimpanzees are found there are also many kinds of monkeys, including baboons. In some places they share the forests with the largest of the ape family, the gorillas. Then there are various kinds of forest antelopes, such as bushbuck and little duikers as well as bush pigs, or giant forest hogs. And, of course, there are hundreds of species of smaller mammals, birds, reptiles, and insects.

Though they usually feed on fruits and leaves, chimpanzees are quite good hunters and, like people, sometimes hunt in groups and cooperate. But most of the time they pay little attention to other animals. And the other animals usually ignore the chimps, too. Sometimes young chimps and young baboons play together, despite the fact that adult male chimps occasionally hunt infant baboons.

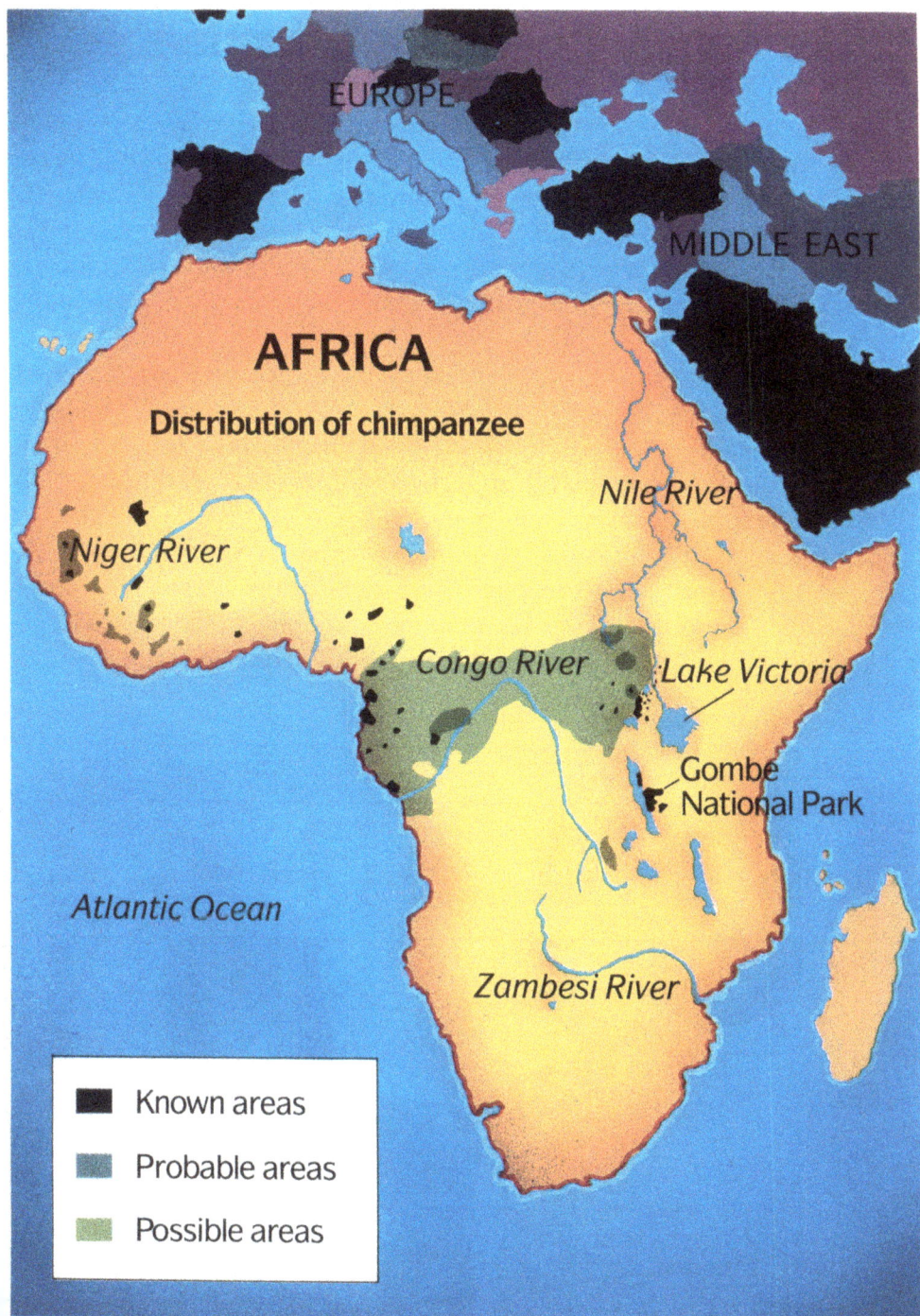

EUROPE

MIDDLE EAST

AFRICA

Distribution of chimpanzee

Nile River

Niger River

Congo River

Lake Victoria

Gombe
National Park

Atlantic Ocean

Zambesi River

◼	Known areas
◼	Probable areas
◼	Possible areas

◇ The Family Tree of the Chimpanzee

The chimpanzee, whose scientific name is *Pan troglodytes* (pan trog-low-*die*-tees), is a primate. The primate family includes galagos (bush babies), lemurs, monkeys, apes, and humans. Chimpanzees are apes—manlike creatures with no tails. Other apes are bonobos (that used to be called pygmy chimpanzees), gorillas, orangutans, and gibbons. Today the largest primates are humans and apes, but there used to be huge monkeys in prehistoric times.

The primates descended from small, insect-eating mammals that lived about fifty million years ago. Gradually some of the primates grew larger and their brains became bigger. They became more and more intelligent. Apes and humans descended from a common ancestor sometime within the last fifteen to twenty million years.

Chimpanzees are more like us than any other creatures alive today. Humans have been able to receive blood transfusions from chimpanzee donors. Their brains look very like ours and, as a result, their intelligence is humanlike too. And in many ways they often behave very much as we do.

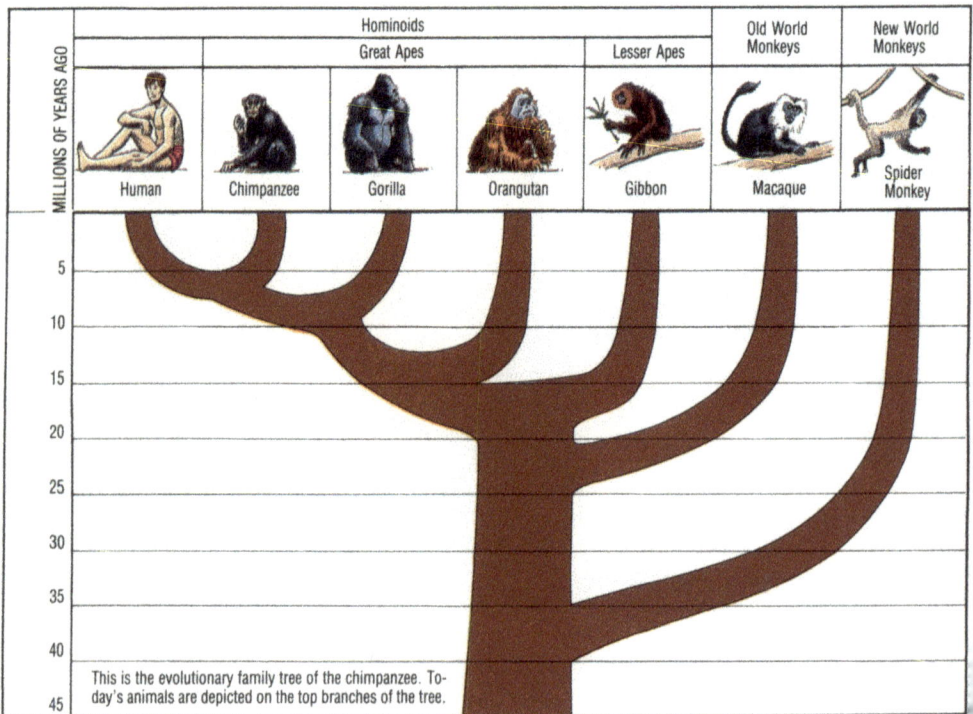

This is the evolutionary family tree of the chimpanzee. To-day's animals are depicted on the top branches of the tree.

◇ The Chimpanzee Community

Chimpanzees live in social groups of up to eighty members. We call such a group a *community*. All the members of a community know each other, and may spend peaceful time together. But the chimpanzee community is very different from the social group of most other primates. Monkeys and gorillas, for example, live in *troops*. All those troop members sleep in the same place, and they all travel around together during the day.

Much of the time chimpanzees move about in small groups that are continually changing. Some chimps in the community only meet occasionally. Others spend a lot of time together and are real friends. A mother and her younger children (up to the age of about seven or eight years) are always together. They may sleep and travel quite by themselves. During a typical day a small family group like this will spend time with other members of the community. But after a while the mother usually leaves the others and moves off with just her family.

Male chimpanzees enjoy each other's company and often travel about in all-male groups. But, every so often, a male leaves the others and spends time by himself or with a chosen friend—who may be his brother.

Male chimpanzees usually work very hard to become high ranking. The top, or *alpha*, male is not usually the biggest or the most aggressive. He gets to the top partly because he is very determined to do so, partly because

he uses his brains. One chimpanzee I knew, called Mike, learned to charge around hitting and kicking empty kerosene cans ahead of him. He got them from my camp. The other males were scared of this noise and rushed to pay their respects to Mike when he stopped. He never had to fight at all. Sometimes, though, males fight each other quite fiercely when they are competing for top rank.

Females are almost always lower ranking than males. They have their own rank order, but it is always changing. A mother will be able to intimidate other females more easily if she is with her adult son or daughter, either of whom will help.

So long as their rank order is stable, chimpanzees seldom fight really seriously. Most of their squabbles are settled by threatening gestures. They wave their arms, swagger upright with bristling hair, give loud barklike calls. The lower-ranked individual gives way and a fight is avoided. Of course, they do fight sometimes—as when males compete for social rank. And they may fight over food or sexual partners. Females get involved in fighting most often when protecting their youngsters.

When the members of the same community fight each other—by hitting, biting, or kicking—this seldom results in bad wounds. But when they are protecting their territory, males may gang up and attack chimpanzees of neighboring communities very brutally. The victims may be hurt so badly that they die.

◇ Sizing Up the Chimpanzee

A fully grown male chimpanzee is about four feet tall and weighs up to 106 pounds. A female is about as tall, but does not weigh more than 92 pounds. Chimpanzees at Gombe are somewhat shorter and lighter. And chimps are often heavier in captivity—at least when they are well kept and given medicine. They have much less exercise, of course.

The bonobos (pygmy chimpanzees) measure up to three feet nine inches tall and weigh up to 100 pounds.

Measurement: height

Lemur
1½ feet

Macaque
22 inches

Gorilla
5½ feet

Orangutan
4½ feet

Chimpanzee
4 feet

Bonobo
3 feet, 9 inches

◇ How Chimpanzees Move

Chimpanzees typically travel from one place to another on the ground. They walk—or run—on all fours. They place the soles of their feet on the ground as we do. But unlike monkeys, they don't use the palms of their hands for walking, but the backs of the second joints of their fingers.

Chimpanzees spend a lot of time in the trees, climbing from branch to branch as they feed. Sometimes they swing from place to place, hand over hand. This is called *brachiating*. All the apes can brachiate, and we can too, but it is much harder for us because our fingers are not long or strong enough. In fact it is altogether harder for us to move about in trees because our feet cannot grip the branches like the feet of the apes, which are really like extra hands.

Chimpanzees sometimes walk upright, although usually for only short distances. They do this when they are carrying things in both hands, or

when they want to look over long grass. Sometimes they walk upright when it is raining—they seem to hate putting their hands on wet ground. Two chimpanzees I knew at Gombe learned to walk upright for long distances after they each had one arm paralyzed by polio. Chimpanzees are so like us that they can catch all our diseases.

Chimpanzee foot

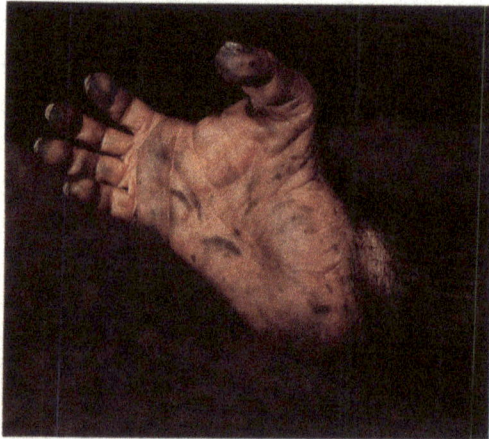

Chimpanzee hand

◇ How Chimpanzees Communicate

Chimpanzees cannot speak to each other as we can. But they have many different calls that all mean different things. Each chimp has his or her own special voice, so everyone knows who is calling. There is, for example, the pant-hoot, a loud sound that carries over long distances. There is a loud spine-chilling *wraaaa* that means danger. And a soft *hoo* is given by an unhappy individual—for example, by a child whose mother won't allow him to nurse when she's weaning him. There are at least thirty-four different calls.

Chimpanzees also communicate with each other by using gestures and body positions. We do, too. We call it "body language." A low-ranking individual greets a superior with a bow, or by crouching in front of him, facing away (this is called *presenting*). An outstretched hand is used to beg for food. An upright swagger is a threat. And so on. Touching is very important. Frightened chimps hold hands or hug each other. Friends may kiss or embrace when they greet.

Social grooming, when chimpanzees move their fingers gently through each other's hair, cleaning the skin, is particularly soothing. Male chimpanzees spend hours doing this, and it helps them to stay friendly even though they sometimes fight. They need to be friendly because they may have to help each other to protect their joint territory.

Chimpanzees have emotions—such as happiness and sadness, anxiety and fear—just as we do. Often you can tell a lot about the mood of a chimp just by watching the expressions on his or her face. Low-ranking chimps watch high-ranking ones carefully and get out of the way if they see signs of irritation or anger.

◇ The Mind of the Chimpanzee

Animals are much smarter than scientists used to think. I used to be told at school that animals (non-human animals, that is) couldn't think or reason, couldn't feel pain, and didn't have their own special characters or emotions. Of course, any of us who have owned a dog or cat, or spent time just watching animals, knows that none of that is true.

It *is* true that the more developed an animal's brain, the more intelligent it is. We have the most developed brain of all, and the great apes, particularly the chimpanzees, have brains very much like ours. Chimpanzees, in fact, can do many things that we used to think only humans could do.

One of the first exciting things I saw at Gombe was how a chimpanzee—David Greybeard—used grass as a tool to "fish" termites from their underground nest. He even made a tool by stripping leaves off a twig so that it would fit in the tunnel. Since then I have seen termite fishing thousands of times. And chimps use other kinds of tools. They use them to solve problems such as how to drink water that has been collected in a tree hollow that cannot be reached with the lips (by using leaves as a sponge and sucking water off that).

Scientists have found out more about the chimpanzee's mind by giving them all kinds of tests. Now we know that they can reason things out. If a banana is out of reach, beyond bars, they will go find a stick to pull in the fruit. They have excellent memories. They can recognize themselves in mirrors.

A chimp named Dar signs "smile."

Chimpanzees can be taught to do all kinds of things that people do—like riding bicycles and smoking. They love to paint. But they cannot learn to speak a human language. Two scientists brought up a little chimp called Vicki and tried to teach her to say words. After eight years she could say only four words—and only people who knew her could understand those. We know that chimpanzees' throats are a bit different from ours. They can't make a lot of our sounds.

Then two other scientists had another idea and this one worked. They taught the sign language that deaf people use to a young chimp named Washoe. She learned over 300 signs. She even invented signs of her own. She called a fizzing soda a "listen drink" (two signs she knew), a piece of celery "pipe food," a duck on a pond "water bird," and so on. Her adopted son learned fifty-eight words from Washoe and three other signing chimps by the time he was eight years old. He never saw humans make these signs.

Other chimpanzees have been taught computer "language" and can punch out quite complicated sentences. At last it is possible to actually "talk" to animals. And they can talk to us. These experiments have taught us a great deal about the chimpanzee mind.

◇ Being Born

A female chimpanzee becomes sexually interesting to the adult males when she is about ten years old. Every twenty-eight days or so she develops a pink swelling on her rear end. It lasts for about ten days and is a sign for the males that she is ready for mating. She does not form a bond with one male for life, but mates with all the males of her community.

When she is twelve or thirteen years old, she becomes pregnant for the first time. About eight months later she gives birth. She usually has her baby when she is alone, and usually at night in her nest.

In the wild most females know how to care for their babies because they have watched other mothers and, unless they were last born in a family, have been able to play with, groom, and carry their brothers and sisters. There was one chimp at Gombe called Fifi whom I first got to know as an infant. When she had her first baby she was a wonderful mother right from the start. She knew exactly what to do when little Freud nuzzled about her breast making little *hoo* sounds—she helped him so that he could reach her breast and suckle. For the first few days she helped him to cling underneath her as she traveled or climbed, supporting his back with one hand. Soon he could hang on by himself. If other chimps came too close, fascinated by the new baby, she either threatened them or moved away.

In captivity, when females are taken very early from their mothers and brought up by humans, or with other babies in "nurseries," they don't have a chance to watch other mothers and babies. When they have babies of their own, they don't know what to do. Then the babies have to be taken away—which means that when they grow up they don't know how to be mothers either. And so it goes on.

◇ Growing Up

I have watched many infant chimpanzees growing up in the wild at Gombe. Freud was quite typical. For five years he suckled, shared his mother's nest at night, and clung to her when she traveled. At first he always rode beneath her. When he was five months old he began to ride on her back. About the same time he took his first tottering steps and climbed his first branches.

Fifi was a particularly good mother—just like her mother Flo had been. She often played with Freud. Some mothers are much less attentive, much less tolerant, much less playful. Once Freud had learned to walk and climb he was anxious to play with others, including adult males. Infants learn a lot during play—about the characters of other infants, about how to leap quickly through the branches.

Freud also learned by watching and then imitating what the others did, especially Fifi. He ate what she ate, in the same way. He practiced using grass tools when she was fishing for termites. He learned what was frightening and how to behave in all sorts of different situations. He learned a lot from experience. When he made a mistake he was sometimes punished. If, for example, he went too close to a male who was in a bad mood he got threatened, even hit.

Freud was very upset when Fifi began to wean him—when she would not let him suckle or ride on her back. But gradually he got used to the idea that he was no longer a baby. When he was five years old his brother Frodo was born. And Freud, like almost all older brothers and sisters, was fascinated by the new baby. As soon as Fifi allowed him to, he began to play with, groom, and carry Frodo.

And then, when Frodo was five years old, Fifi gave birth to Fanni. The next baby after Fanni was Flossi, and she quickly became the spoiled baby of the family.

Fifi gradually became higher ranking as she got older. She helped Freud when, at the age of eight, he began to challenge the females of the community. And so he was able to get the better of them when he was quite young. For the other youngsters with lower ranking and more timid mothers, life is much harder. When Freud was ten years old he began to challenge lower-ranking adult males. He had begun the long struggle to get a high position in the community.

22

◇ Living Day to Day

Gradually the moonlight changes to the gray light of dawn. High above me there is a rustling of leaves. That is where, the night before, I left Fifi and infant Flossi. All over Gombe chimpanzees are beginning to wake up, moving sleepily in their leafy beds. And all over Africa, wherever there are chimps, they will be getting ready to start a new day.

For chimpanzees every day is different from the one before. And each chimpanzee is quite different, in character and behavior, from every other chimpanzee. I have picked a day in Fifi's life that is a fairly typical one. Other chimps throughout their forest homes will often have days like this.

As it gets lighter, Fifi moves again and idly grooms Flossi, who has snuggled close to suckle. There are more rustling sounds and Fanni, who is now eight years old, swings from her little nest nearby, climbs over to Fifi and, holding her arms up, asks to be groomed. Fifi sits up, yawns, then the two groom while Flossi gets in the way. But she is not punished.

Presently Fifi climbs down and moves off through the undergrowth, Flossi clinging to her back. Fanny follows and I crawl and wriggle after them. Soon Fifi climbs a tree full of ripe figs. And there, feeding overhead, we find Fifi's older offspring, Frodo, now an adolescent of thirteen years, and Freud, who is eighteen years old now and quite grown up. They all grunt, pleased to see each other. Fanni runs to kiss Freud's head and he touches her back in a gentle greeting. Flossi goes to Frodo and jumps into his lap to be hugged.

Suddenly there are sounds in the undergrowth and three adult males appear, followed by another mother and child. When Fifi and her family see them they give loud pant-hoots and Freud rushes down to greet one of them, the alpha male, Goblin. But before he gets there Goblin and the other two start charging about below the tree, dragging branches and hurling rocks. Freud, screaming in fear, rushes back towards Fifi. Goblin kicks the wide buttresses of a huge forest tree, making a drumming sound. The other two males do the same. Then they calm down, their display of strength over, and climb to feed.

Fifi and Frodo hurry to greet them with soft panting sounds. Fifi crouches before Goblin, who embraces them. Frodo grooms one of the other males. But Freud, who is very frightened of Goblin, quietly leaves the tree and goes off by himself. The others settle to feeding—except Fanni, Flossi, and the

newly arrived child. They prefer to play, chasing through the branches and tickling each other, uttering grunts and chuckles of chimpanzee laughter.

When the adults have eaten all they want they climb down, one by one, and stretch out on the ground. Frodo hero-worships Goblin and he grooms him. One of the other males grooms Fifi.

An hour later they all move off together. Flossi sits upright on Fifi like a little jockey. Suddenly we hear the birdlike calls of red colobus monkeys above us in the canopy. The male chimps are excited. They reach out and touch each other, their hair bristling. Then they climb and start to hunt. It is Frodo who succeeds in snatching a tiny infant monkey from its mother. But Goblin races through the branches and seizes Frodo's catch for himself. With a quick bite Goblin kills the prey. Screaming loudly, Frodo begs for a share with outstretched hand. Goblin threatens him angrily and, screaming even louder, poor Frodo goes off with nothing.

Goblin shares some of his meat with the other males when they approach and beg. And he lets Fifi pull off a large piece. She moves away to enjoy it, chewing each mouthful slowly along with a handful of leaves. Frodo and Fanni follow and beg from her. She lets them take the chewed, meaty-tasting leaves from her mouth. Flossi is allowed to suck on the meat itself.

When the meat is finished, the group breaks up. Frodo goes off with Goblin and the other males. Fifi and her daughters travel with the other mother, whose son is about the same age as Flossi. Presently Fifi finds an underground bees' nest. She breaks off a thick stick to enlarge the opening, then, ignoring the angry bees, reaches in and scoops out a handful of honey. The other females take some. They run off, away from the bees, to enjoy this rare feast. The small infants stay well away when their mothers raid the nest, but they share the honey afterwards.

By evening Fifi is once more on her own with her daughters. They climb for the last meal of the day—bright yellow blossoms.

And then it is time for sleep. Fifi chooses two parallel branches and bends lots of smaller branches over them. She puts soft leafy twigs under her head and lies on this comfortable, springy bed. Flossi moves beside her mother and suckles. Fanni makes her own nest nearby.

Throughout the forests of Africa the chimpanzees have settled down to sleep after a long, busy day. In some places it will be raining and they will be miserable and cold. But the chimps in Gombe have two months before *their* wet season begins.

Just as I am about to leave Fifi I hear, from the deep forest, the pant-hoot of a single male. I recognize the voice—it's Freud. Fifi and Fanni call in reply and, from further away, other chimps join in, their voices swelling into a musical chorus. Then they fall silent as the dusk gives way to the tropical night.

◇ Chimpanzees in Captivity

The first chimpanzees were brought to Europe from Africa in the middle of the seventeenth century. People were amazed by these humanlike creatures. They dressed them up and taught them tricks.

Since then we have treated chimpanzees like slaves, sending them to zoos, selling them for pets, training them to perform in the circus and movies. Some chimps became famous. J. Fred Muggs starred in TV's *Today Show* for years and was known by millions of viewers. And a young male called Ham became the first American astronaut. He was shot up in a Mercury Redstone rocket in January 1961. Because he survived the ordeal, it was decided that it was safe for the first human to go into space.

Today there are about five thousand chimpanzees in captivity around the world. And hundreds of them are treated very badly indeed. Many trainers beat their chimps to make them perform. When Ham was taught what to do in his flight into space he got an electric shock every time he touched the wrong button.

Infant chimpanzees are cute and cuddly. People can buy them and treat them like human children. But once they get big they may bite. They don't want to be dressed up and told what to do all the time. Then their "parents" don't want them, and send them to zoos or laboratories.

Zoos are mostly much better than they used to be, but there are still many chimps in small concrete and metal cages with no trees to climb and nothing to play with. The best zoos keep their chimpanzees in groups and provide them with all kinds of interesting things to do—different things every day so they don't get bored.

Because they are so like us, chimpanzees are used by scientists to try and find out more about human diseases and how to cure or prevent them. Chimpanzees can be infected with almost all human diseases. Today they are being used in AIDS research. So far, though, no chimp has shown any symptoms of AIDS. Even though chimpanzees are being forced to dedicate their lives to helping humans, they are almost never given nice living conditions. Hundreds of them are shut up in tiny, bare steel-barred prisons, all by themselves, sad and utterly bored.

A group called the Committee for Conservation and Care of Chimpanzees is working very hard to make things better for all chimpanzees in captivity.

◇ Protecting Chimpanzees

Chimpanzees in the wild are disappearing very fast. Just fifty years ago there were millions of them. They were found in the forests of at least twenty-five countries throughout equatorial Africa. Now there are only about 150,000 to 200,000. And they exist only in scattered populations. They have become extinct in four nations, and in only five areas of Central Africa are they found in anything like their original numbers.

They are disappearing for various reasons. In some places they are killed for food. In most countries they are illegally hunted for sale to animal dealers who send them to zoos, circuses, or laboratories, or sell them as pets. The dealers only want young chimps—the adults are too big and dangerous to handle. So the hunters usually shoot the mothers to take away their babies. Often several mothers and even male chimpanzees must be shot in order to capture one baby that is not too badly wounded. Many babies die in the long journey to their final destination.

Finally, the chimpanzees are vanishing because their forest homes are being destroyed. All over Africa, trees are felled to make way for farms and villages and roads, or to be sold as timber for greedy buyers from the developed world.

If more people do not try to help, soon chimpanzees will be almost gone in the wild, living only in a few protected areas. We must work hard to set up new parks and reserves where they can live safely. It would be terrible if we sat back and allowed our closest relatives to vanish from the world.

About the Author

JANE GOODALL was born in London on April 3, 1934, and grew up in Bournemouth, on the southern coast of England. In 1960, she began studying chimpanzees in the wild in Gombe, Tanzania. After receiving her doctorate in ethology at Cambridge University, Dr. Goodall founded the Gombe Stream Research Center for the study of chimpanzees and baboons. In 1977, she established the Jane Goodall Institute for Wildlife Research, Education and Conservation to promote animal research throughout the world. She has written three books for adults, including the bestseller *In the Shadow of Man*, and three books for children, including the recent *My Life With the Chimpanzees* and *The Chimpanzee Family Book*.

Jane Goodall's commitment to the animal world is expressed in her words, "Only when we understand can we care. Only when we care can we help. Only when we help shall they be saved." You can learn more about joining in her efforts to protect endangered wildlife by contacting

The Jane Goodall Institute
1120 20th St NW
Washington, DC 20036
Phone: (703) 682-9220

Published by iBooks an imprint of
J. Boylston & Company, Publishers
Produced by Byron Preiss Visual Publications, Inc.
Manhanset House
POB 342
Dering Harbor NY 11965
bricktower@aol.com • www.ibooksinc.com

Cover photo copyright © by Photo Researchers, Inc.
Back cover photo copyright © by Vanne Goodall
Front cover photo insert of Jane Goodall by Hugo Van Lawick copyright © National Geographic Society
Introduction photo of Jane Goodall copyright © Ben Asen
Interior illustrations copyright © 1989 by Byron Preiss Visual Publications, Inc.

Interior photos copyright © by Jane Goodall, except for the following: page 1 copyright © George Holton/Photo Researchers, Inc.; page 12 (top) copyright © H. Albrecht/Bruce Coleman, Inc.; page 12 (bottom, left) copyright © Toni Angermayer/Photo Researchers, Inc.; page 12 (bottom, right) copyright © Dr. Gregory G. Dimijian/Photo Researchers, Inc.; page 13 (right) copyright © Tom McHugh/Photo Researchers, Inc.; and page 16 (right) page 29 copyright © Bernard Pierre Wolfe/Photo Researchers, Inc.; pages 7, 8, 14 (top), 18 (right) and 27 copyright © Baron Hugo Van Lawick; pages 17 and 30 copyright © Deborah H. Fouts/Friends of Washoe.

Data for map on page 5 courtesy of Geza Teleki, George Washington University, Washington, D.C., and the Survival Service Commission of the International Union for the Conservation of Nature and Natural Resources

Interior illustrations by Ralph Reese
Map by Rurick Tyler

Special thanks to Judy Wilson, Jonathan Lanman, Judy Johnson, Dr. Geza Teleki, and Dr. Mary Ellen Morbeck.

Editor: Ruth Ashby
Associate Editor: Gwendolyn Smith
Cover design: Ted Mader & Associates
Interior design: Alex Jay/Studio J